THE
WILDFLOWER

VICKI M. BOOTH

www.xulonpress.com

Blessings Stephanie,

Love,
Karen
12/15

DEDICATION

To my sons:

Christian,
Jonathan,
and Austin

"I keep asking that the God of our Lord Jesus Christ, the glorious Father, may give you the Spirit of wisdom and revelation, so that you may know Him better." —Ephesians 1:17

To my husband:

Michael,
lover, healer, friend

*"Many waters cannot quench love;
rivers cannot wash it away.
If one were to give
all the wealth of his house for love,
it would be utterly scorned."*
—Song of Songs 8:7

TABLE OF CONTENTS

INTRODUCTION

THE WILDFLOWER

...his compassions fail not. They are new every morning: great is thy faithfulness. —Lamentations 3:22-23 (KJV)

I've done lots of gardening thanks to watching my mother do her share over the years and catching the bug from her. There's something about being outdoors digging in the dirt, planting things, and then watching them grow and bloom that is very satisfying. I landscaped our yard myself, and twice a year I plant lots of annuals. It's fun trying different varieties from season to season to see how well I can get them to grow. I attribute this love of dirt and growing things to our farmer roots; almost all my ancestors on my mother's side were farmers. I also like to think it's as close as one can get to doing the job originally assigned to mankind.

One of the things I've learned in this pursuit is that some plants require a lot of attention and pampering.

Take roses, for example. They need fertilizer, pest and fungus control measures, and exact pruning to do really well. Some of mine have fared very poorly when left on their own and some have fallen slightly short of their full potential when missing just one of these elements. When given all these things at the proper times, roses thrive, become beautiful and are a showpiece in the gardener's yard.

In contrast to the gardener's fine hybrid roses, wildflowers do not receive the slightest help from any human other than the courtesy of not being mown down! Since moving to Tennessee I have been struck with the different varieties and sheer volume of wildflowers that grow here. My oldest son attended a school about 40 minutes away, and while driving him there and back I had the opportunity to see fields upon fields of wildflowers. Often I was amazed at where I saw them growing. Some were on rocky outcrops with little soil and I marveled that they were able get their roots out enough to survive. Some grew in pastures where horses and cows used them for forage, but they managed to grow in spite of that as well.

Once I pulled our van to the side of the road, and my son got out and picked one of the wildflowers for me to see the size of it and how its petals were constructed. I have designs on doing a painting of wildflowers, so I was always on the lookout for a scenic panorama or field with an old barn surrounded by these colorful blooms. Pink, lavender, yellow, white, and blue. Various shapes and sizes, although none very large. The one thing common to them all was that they weren't pampered or babied; they grew in spite of having sporadic rain, zero pest and fungus control, or any type of human interference. Yet the ultimate gardener, God Himself, cared for these wildflowers. "... Consider the lilies of the field, how they grow; they toil not, neither do they spin: and yet I say unto you, that even Solomon in all his glory was not arrayed like one of these." Matt. 6:28,29.

Now all this talk about gardening and flowers originates from the following: my husband, Michael, and I flew out to California to see a counselor who helped us tremendously in the areas in which we were struggling. The illustrations that I have been using about the rose and the wildflower are actually her illustrations and were the method she used in getting me to see something about myself. What she related to us was how some people are planned and very much wanted before their birth. She called these individuals roses. They grow close to the door of the gardener's home and receive from him the attention necessary to become all that they can be. Then she explained that there are those who are not planned. They are the wildflowers growing out in the field that have no gardener. No one comes to fertilize or water them. Sometimes they endure periods of drought or careless breaking and biting by animals. They must rely on God alone to receive all that is necessary for their survival. But they do survive and continue as witnesses of the Creator and His mercy merely by the fact that they remain.

Because of how I entered this world, I am a wildflower, cared for by God, without ever having the benefit of a human father to counsel, guide, and protect me. And if my suspicions are correct, there are many of you out there who are wildflowers too. It is to you and for you that I am writing this book. Within it I hope to give voice to your feelings as well as my own, as all too often being unplanned, or illegitimate, is a subject not talked about within the community of believers.

I have examined and re-examined my motives for writing this because what they are is very important to me. Sometimes I think my reasons have been selfish because I enjoy writing and want to be able to feel like I am doing something worthwhile. At some intervals I have thought my motives are to identify with others in similar situations and offer helpful insights; at others to just vent, and others to address an issue I feel is rarely if ever addressed. However, the best motive, the one I would most like to be true, is to bring glory to God and to show how He can work through sinful people and situations to bring about good.

What I would most like for you, dear reader, to take away from this book is this: my story is not one of tragedy, but of triumph; it is not my triumph, but God's. Jesus is the Supreme Overcomer, and through Him we may also overcome.

VICKI AND HER MOTHER, MARTHA

CHAPTER 1

ILLEGITIMATE

*But God has chosen the foolish things
of the world to put to shame the wise,
and God has chosen the weak things
of the world to put to shame the things
which are mighty; and the base things
of the world and the things which
are despised God has chosen, and
the things which are not, to bring to
nothing the things which are, that no
flesh should glory in His presence.*
—1 Corinthians 1:27-29

I remember encountering the term "illegitimate" for the first time when I saw a court document related to my child support. My mother had inadvertently left it lying where I could see it. I didn't know what the term meant, but in spite of my ignorance I had a funny feeling in the pit of my stomach that it couldn't mean anything good, and I knew that the term was referring to me. From then on I found myself frequently feeling that there was something not good about me, and how I came to be here. I knew that not having a father who was married to my mother was somehow not within the proper way of doing things even though I had no idea that it also violated God's rules. It's intriguing to me that this demonstrates that God has written His law on the hearts of men (Romans 2:15).

When I was a very young child nothing seemed out of the ordinary in my family. Since my birth, my mother and I had lived with my grandparents out of necessity. At such a tender age, I didn't know that was not exactly considered normal. But the older I grew, the more I took notice of the families that were in my life. I saw that my two cousins, both girls, had a mom and a dad. I noticed that my neighbors had moms and dads. And I noticed the same thing with my classmates. I was even teased by some of the neighbor children for not having a dad. My mother worked as a teacher aid at my elementary school where we were both looked down upon by some individuals. All these things reinforced the idea that I wasn't supposed to be born in the way that I was, or perhaps be born at all.

Before I was a teenager, I was made aware that my father had outright rejected me, and that he had even tried talking my mother into aborting me. This was before abortion was legal, and he was a doctor. As such he was fully aware of the development of preborn babies, and that they are not just blobs of tissue. I thought that made him even more guilty of attempted murder than if he had been ignorant of the facts. His denial of even my right to live seemed particularly heinous because of his medical knowledge.

Around age 15, I started dating a guy whose father I really took a liking to because he treated me as if I were his daughter. He once told me that someone had said to him, "But don't you know *who* she is?" He said that he replied, "Yes, and I don't give a darn." Now that may have seemed like a nice thing for him to do, taking up for me and all, but in reality it only served to, once again, drive home the point that I was illegitimate and somehow a second class citizen because of it.

In the years since becoming an adult I've had the opportunity to study people in the Bible who were illegitimate. In the Old Testament, I found that being illegitimate disqualified people from serving God in certain capacities which mainly had to do with the Levitical priesthood; however, one of Israel's judges, Jephthah, was illegitimate. Judges 11:1,2 states: Jephthah the Gileadite was a mighty warrior. His father was Gilead; his mother was a prostitute. Gilead's wife also bore him sons, and when they were grown up, they drove Jephthah away. "You are not going to get any inheritance in our family," they said, "because you are the son of another woman."

But that isn't the end of the story. Jephthah fled and went to live in another place called Tob. He must have been pretty charismatic, though, because a "group of adventurers" began to gather around him and follow him. They apparently raided the neighboring peoples, bringing themselves a good bit of fame in the process.

Eventually an amazing turn of events occurred: the very ones who drove him away came to him, wanting him to lead them in battle against their enemies with a promise to make him ruler over them if he agreed. The Lord made Jephthah successful in all his battles, and the Bible even says the Spirit of the Lord came upon him to enable him to defeat the Ammonites. This unlikely hero led Israel six years. I suppose the worst thing he did was to make a rash vow concerning sacrificing the first thing that met him at his door after his huge victory. Tragically it turned out to be his only child, a daughter. This makes me wonder exactly what he expected to come out of his house!

The next person, or rather people, who come to mind are Judah and Tamar's twins. This account is found in Genesis 38. Judah got a wife for his son, Er, and the Lord put Er to death because he was wicked. According to their custom, Judah attempted to have the next brother in line marry and sleep with Tamar so that she would become pregnant with an heir for the dead son. However, Onan did not fulfill this duty, so the Lord put him to death also. Judah didn't want a repeat with the next boy so he withheld him from her. She ended up pretending to be a prostitute, became pregnant by Judah himself and gave birth to Perez and Zerah. The Bible says he never knew her again, which means she did not become his wife. According to the genealogy of Jesus in Matthew, Perez became an ancestor of the Messiah, Jesus. This man's illegitimacy didn't stop God from using him in the lineage of the Redeemer.

There remains one more Person who was perceived by some as being illegitimate: Jesus Himself. Nothing is further from the truth, but to some of the residents in Mary and Joseph's little hometown, His origins must have seemed less than proper. Even Joseph had to be convinced by a heavenly messenger that Mary hadn't fooled around on him. It's an intriguing thought that Jesus probably had to deal with the whispers and gossip of people who realized He was not Joseph's son, but did not realize He was God's son. He knows what it's like to be judged by others in the same way I have been judged, and it is a comforting thing to know that the God of the Universe knows how I feel due to His personal experience.

What studying this subject in the Bible taught me is that God uses anyone He chooses, regardless of their pedigree or how they got here, in making His plans succeed. Our past doesn't have to determine our future. And if we are regenerated and have repented of our sin, God views us as being as righteous as Jesus (2

Corinthians 5:21). Through God's plan He exchanged the believers' unrighteousness for His righteousness. We are no longer illegitimate children, but ours is the adoption as sons (and daughters) into the family of God (Ephesians 1:5). Although I am legally illegitimate in regard to fleshly things, I nor any other born again believer is spiritually illegitimate (Galatians 3:26). This is something for which we can be truly thankful.

I've also learned that when Jesus came in the flesh, He truly experienced the same types of pain we as humans must endure in order to become an understanding High Priest for us. Hebrews 2:10 says: "In bringing many sons to glory, it was fitting that God, for whom and through whom everything exists, should make the author of their salvation perfect through suffering." This included, among other things, being perceived as being illegitimate.

CHAPTER 2

SIN INTO BLESSING

*And we know that in all things God
works for the good of those who love
Him, who have been called according
to His purpose. —Romans 8:28*

Once I heard a radio show where a pastor said that babies born out of wedlock are not blessings from God. At first I was more than a little offended given my background, but after I heard him out I had to agree. God is not going to bless the sins of fornication or adultery. It goes against His character. However, this does not mean that God will not choose to bring good out of any situation. Let me explain...

Before I was born my grandfather was an alcoholic for many years. This led to many terrible events in his life and the life of the family. He once caused an accident while driving drunk; he physically harmed my grandmother by pulling out a large patch of her hair in a drunken rage, and she bit his earlobe off during their struggle; yet again while drunk he tried to kill my mother by bashing her head in with a six-foot level while she was pregnant with me, but she was able to put her hands up and catch it before it hit her. My mother always exclaims, "The bottle got that house", in reference to the nice home they lost; he also lost his furniture making business and ended up alienated from my grandmother, mother, and uncle. Finally they decided to send him to Bay Pines, a veteran's hospital in Tampa, in order to get him "dried out". This happened shortly before I arrived on the scene.

During the time in which he was at Bay Pines, he decided that he wanted to come home before his next grandchild was born. Something (or Someone) was at work within his heart. He phoned my mother and grandmother and said, "I want to come home so badly before that baby is born." I was due on December 25, 1968. I ended up being born on December 30, but not before my grandfather got his wish. He came home from Bay Pines never to take a drink again. And instead of the little black haired boy he'd wanted, he ended up with a little blonde haired girl.

My grandfather's life as a drunk was turned around by the birth of an illegitimate baby. He had two older, legitimate granddaughters from my uncle and aunt, but neither of their births effected the change in him that my birth did. I was the only baby for whom he'd ever changed diapers—and they were cloth back then! Despite his painful arthritis he would get down on the floor and play games with me, letting me win, of course! I remember him allowing me to go out into his garden with him where he would cut off long stalks of sugar cane and peel and cut smaller pieces for me to chew until the sweet was gone. When we came in from being in the garden, he would always say, "Shew!" and I would try my best to imitate him.

Once he found a two-foot-long alligator out in the yard (one of the perils of living in Florida) and caught it and put it in a washtub. I was scared to death of it. He teased me about being afraid of it but not my little rubber alligators that I carried with me just about everywhere. I'd go to the hardware store with him where he'd let me run my hands through the various bins of bolts and nuts to my heart's content. I also remember being carried around by him much of the time. Whenever I'd wake up in the mornings with my eyes all blurry, I'd go and sit with him in his chair, rubbing them until they cleared up and I could see.

All this seems wonderful, but the story gets better. I used to play with a little New Testament Bible like the ones the Gideons give out. My grandfather saw me with it and how it would frequently end up inside my toy box.

One day he asked my mother to get it out for him, but she was in a hurry to leave and told him she would do it when she got back. While she was gone, he decided to dig through the toy box himself and get it. When she arrived home, she found him reading that little New Testament, so when she had the chance she went and bought him a large print Bible. From reading that Bible my grandfather, realizing he needed to be saved, repented and accepted Jesus' payment for his sin. He passed from this life into Glory when I was just five years old.

It's amazing what God can and does use to save people. My grandfather's conversion reminds me of the account of Joseph, who when speaking to his brothers when he was second in command to Pharaoh said, "Do not be afraid, for am I in the place of God? But as for you, you meant evil against me, but God meant it for good, in order to bring it about as it is this day, to save many people alive." Although not initially sent as a blessing but the result of a sinful act, God turned the birth of an illegitimate child into a blessing "to save" at least one person "alive".

VICKI'S GRANDFATHER HOLDING HER
AS AN INFANT, AND HER COUSIN.

CHAPTER 3

BEAUTY INSTEAD OF ASHES

*...to give unto them beauty for ashes,
the oil of joy for mourning, the garment
of praise for the spirit of heaviness.*
—Isaiah 61:3 (KJV)

From the time I had my first real boyfriend, to whom I eventually became engaged, I believed I could not survive without a guy in my life. That engagement was broken about a year after it had begun. Following that I was consistently in some kind of dating relationship with various young men, desperately chasing the male attention I'd always lacked. The one thing most of these jokers—er, guys had in common was that at the time they were not great husband material.

Most of them claimed to be Christians but were not living in a very convincing manner, but then again neither was I. I won't judge whether they were or not because only they and the Lord truly know the answer. The evidence was sorely lacking for most of them, until I met one young man who was different. He was preparing to enter the ministry and he was the first guy I found who seemed completely surrendered to God's will. Ironically, we met shortly after I'd told God I didn't believe guys like him existed. I feel that God arranged that meeting for two purposes: to get me out of a bad relationship I'd been in for two years, and to show me that godly young men did exist. Even though my life was a mess and my heart had been broken repeatedly, I still wished for a relationship with a godly person. Not much happened between the two of us due to his unwillingness to commit, but enough happened to turn my life around. I saw evidence of God's work in that man and from then on I knew that was what I wanted in a spouse. God had proven to me that it was out there.

Now one of the problems with dating Christian men is that some of them use God as an excuse for not forming any attachments (I used to visualize them hiding in the folds at the bottom of some huge figure's robes). I found that they could be quite leery of what I call the "C" word, which stands for commitment. After that first young Christian man, I met and dated another Christian man who was equally noncommittal and used the well-worn "I'm praying for God's will in this matter" line. Apparently it wasn't God's will for us to stay together! He was truly a nice Christian guy but thought he was too old for me, so he broke things off.

After this experience I was absolutely sick of men—any kind of them: lost ones, saved ones, you name it. I was gradually releasing my death grip on my need for a boyfriend. Or maybe God was prying it out of my hands. Either way, I came to the point where I told God that if it just had to be Him and me for the rest of my life, then I was perfectly fine with that. In my mind I can still see, frozen in time, where I was sitting and what I was wearing when this happened. My will was broken, and it felt wonderful! The relief was enormous and at that instant came streaming over me in one healing moment. The burden was finally gone, and I literally felt lighter physically. Ever so patiently, God worked on me during all those years I felt I needed a boyfriend, until he finally brought me to the point where I didn't.

I believe God has a sense of humor, and this is how it manifested itself in my love life. About two weeks after I told the Lord I was fine with just the two of us, one of my friends invited me to attend the Sunday evening service of a church in Tampa with her. She was interested in the first Christian guy I wrote about and was going there to visit because that's where he was serving as the youth pastor. We didn't know that there was a concert scheduled for that evening. We walked in and found some seats near the front left of the building. Later, after the usual welcome and such, three guys got up to sing. We took notice of how nice looking the two younger ones were (the third was their dad), and especially the one standing on our side because he was the one of whom we had the best view. We saw he was wearing a wedding ring, however, so that disqualified him from further inspection! During the intermission, the other one came and introduced himself to us and shook our hands. Immediately after it was over we left because I was beginning to come down with some bug, and I never gave it a second thought.

A week went by and my friend wanted to see the object of her affection again, so she convinced me to attend a New Year's Eve party with her. It was at the University of South Florida and was hosted by Baptist Campus Ministries, of which he was the President. So off we went, driving in circles once we arrived on campus, lost, for about 30 minutes. We almost bailed out but at the last minute we finally located the huge building in which the party was being held. Before we went inside, I hesitated and told my friend I wanted to wait out front for a while so I could size up the situation. I'm not a big fan of crowds, especially large ones. Soon a nice guy came out, spotted us, and invited us to come in, so we headed toward the door. Upon entering, we saw the place was jammed full of college kids who were busy listening to a band, playing ping-pong, talking, or eating.

We caught sight of the President playing ping-pong like a madman and my friend took the opportunity to say hello to him. Next we wandered around until we found some seats in the room with the band. Suddenly my friend leaned over and raised her voice above the blaring music while pointing, "Hey, isn't that the guy that was singing the other night?" I looked in the direction she had gestured, and sure enough it was. He appeared to be there with a friend. So we made our way over to where they were standing and reintroduced ourselves.

I was reminded that his name was Michael Booth, and he told me that he, his brother and dad had recently formed their singing group. I mentioned that I worked as a graphic artist and he said the group needed a logo (little did I know they couldn't afford to pay for one and this was just a ploy to keep the conversation going!). We talked for a while and when we were ready to leave he walked us out to our car. I decided to give him a business card with my work number in case he was serious about the logo.

Two weeks later I received a phone call at work from Michael, only he wasn't contacting me about a logo. Instead, he asked if I would meet him at a church where they were booked to sing next since it was in my town and he needed to check out the sound equipment. I told him I would. After we arrived, he went to the door of the church building and twisted the knob. It was locked. Later on I learned this had been his way of getting to meet again—he had no intention of checking any sound equipment!

He asked me out and I really didn't know what to think, what with me recently surrendering my love life and all. I was feeling very cautious. But I agreed, and for the first time ever I had no expectations. I liked him and I could tell he was a good man. He was sweet and thoughtful. After dating him for a while I started having feelings for him—cautious feelings!

About the same time I started having these feelings three guys emerged, from what seemed like nowhere, professing their great affection for me. The first was an acquaintance who worked for the lawn service that mowed my employer's lawn. He came into my workplace and sang "You Lost That Loving Feeling" to me in front of my coworkers! I was speechless. The next, a former classmate, asked me to meet him at a restaurant to talk. I agreed, and after we were both seated he proceeded to tell me he'd always had a thing for me throughout high school. It sure took him long enough to fess up; this was five years after graduation! Then one of my coworkers clued me in that he had taken a liking to me by parking himself in my cubicle frequently for long periods of time. He eventually asked me out. After the shock from these experiences wore off, my initial thought was, "And where were all of you back when I was dateless?" Then I realized I had a decision to make. Should I keep dating Michael exclusively, or give these others a chance? It didn't require much thought to know the right thing to do was to stick with Michael. I could tell the other three were just the same old thing from before, packaged differently.

A few months after Michael and I began dating exclusively we came to realize we really liked—even loved each other. My relationship with him was very different from all the men who had come before. What I was most attracted to in Michael was the beauty of the presence of God in his life. In my heart I knew he was the one God had intended for me all along. We got engaged over the Thanksgiving Holiday that year, and were married the following April in 1993.

This is how God gave me beauty for ashes. In the middle of the ash heap that was my love life He made me long for His presence. He patiently orchestrated my life to where I finally surrendered my will to Him. Then He dropped the man of my dreams and more into my lap. How God's sense of humor came into play is that when I finally didn't want a man, He gave me one. To this day it makes me smile when I think about it.

A FAVORITE WEDDING PHOTO

Chapter 4

Boy oh Boy!

Sons are a heritage from the Lord, children a reward from Him. Like arrows in the hands of a warrior are sons born in one's youth. Blessed is the man whose quiver is full of them.
—*Psalm 127:3-5*

Our quiver is definitely full of boys! Remember that sense of humor I said I believe God has? More than once in my life this has become very apparent, but not more than when He decided to give the girl who'd grown up without much male interaction in her life a husband, and then one, two, and finally three boys.

Our first little arrow, who is now a huge teenager, we decided to name Christian Michael. He was born in 1995 on December 30. What a wonderful birthday present to me—I believe God did that to remind me that he was a gift! He burst onto the scene telling us exactly how he thought things should be, and that hasn't changed a bit.

When Christian was two, he started asking for a baby. So we told him he needed to pray and ask God because God is the one who makes babies. We prayed every night with him, and about ten months after we began praying we found out Jonathan David was on the way. After a somewhat difficult pregnancy in which we were concerned he might not make it, he was born a month early on July 10, 1999, weighing just 5 lbs. 11 oz. The little guy was so small he couldn't keep himself warm, and I would wrap him up inside my bathrobe on top of my chest to make sure he was toasty enough. He was a sweet baby who has grown into a kindhearted boy.

Shortly after moving into our first Tennessee home we suffered an early miscarriage. After that we thought we were done having children, but God wasn't finished adding to our family. In 2006 we found out we were expecting twins. In God's providence, He again decided to take one of those babies to Himself, but He graciously left with us Mr. Personality. Austin Neil made his debut on June 9, 2007. He was due on 7/7/07 but instead came on the birthday of my precious aunt, who had died from breast cancer a couple years before. We have been so blessed by God's little surprise for us, and we have been able to enjoy his shenanigans more than the others due to us not being such uptight parents now that we are older.

Living in a testosterone-permeated home can have its challenges. But God didn't leave me totally unprepared. Growing up I would describe myself as a tomboy; I was never what I would call a girlie girl who had to have her clothing and hair just so—not until I became a teenager, that is. Being outside climbing trees and building forts was my favorite thing to do rather than being inside playing with dolls. I loved catching minnows, lizards, turtles, frogs, bugs, and even non-venomous snakes. I enjoyed riding bikes and archery. Today all this comes in very handy, especially since I homeschool. When we are young we don't see how God is preparing us for our lives ahead, but after we are grown up we can look back and see His hand at work in our likes, dislikes and experiences.

All that preparation doesn't mean I haven't had to learn a thing or two about maleness. When I was little the men's section of the local department store seemed like a fascinating, foreign land, and its items like exotic wares. What was all that manly merchandise, like cufflinks, tie tacks and valets? Any time my mother and I walked through there to enter or exit the store I couldn't stop staring at all the stuff and wondering about its purpose. Since getting married I've been educated about those mysterious items in the men's section thanks to Michael's love of clothing!

Some other things I've learned while gaining all these men are that there will be shouting at the TV during football games and fascination with bodily functions. The most popular reason for building something is so it can be destroyed, demolished, or blown up. Males have a passion for fire and things that explode and a desire to shoot things. They *will* break things, just plan on it. I've also come to the realization that they are far better than me at figuring out electronic gadgets.

Initially I wanted a girl when I became pregnant with Christian, but God knew best. I believe that He gave me only our boys for good reason. I do not think I could have dealt with having a daughter. Not that I wouldn't love any child God chose to give, but I think I would have had an undue amount of jealously toward the relationship she and Michael would have formed. God is so kind to us regarding some things and I believe this was something He knew I couldn't bear and wanted to spare me from it. In spite of the bad He allows to happen in our lives He gives mercies within our trials. I love my boys and having them makes me feel like the queen of my home, with no jealousy of the relationships they have with their father. God cares about those details. As the ultimate parent He knows when to be tough and when His children need special treatment.

VICKI WITH ALL HER BOYS

CHAPTER 5

MYSTERIOUS WAYS

*Oh, the depth of the riches of the
wisdom and knowledge of God! How
unsearchable His judgments, and His
paths beyond tracing out!*
—Romans 11:33

God works in mysterious ways. Who among us has not heard this saying? From experience I have found that it is true. There are a few momentous events in my life that can only be explained by God's direct intervention. They stand out in my mind because they have been the exception rather than the rule.

One of these experiences was in one of my dealings with my father. As I mentioned before, he was a doctor. He was the first to practice medicine in the Brandon/Valrico, Florida area. I finally met him when I was around twelve and had an ailment that prompted my mother to contact him, seeking advice. He asked her to bring me in to see him for treatment (I suspect this was because of him not wanting to pay for someone else to see me rather than because I was his daughter). So she set up an appointment with his office. I was beyond shocked he had offered to see me and very nervous about meeting him.

Before and during the appointment I was very anxious. Our first meeting consisted of purely doctor/patient interaction. He was very aloof and professional, similar to Willie Wonka's dentist father in the movie *Charlie and the Chocolate Factory*—only at least in the movie Willie's father hugged him after realizing who he was.[1] I spoke very little because I didn't know what to say to him. What does a child say to a parent who has denied them when they are brought into that parent's presence? The whole ordeal was extremely awkward.

From that time until I was about the age of 17 I had to see him when I was sick. I never said anything to him at my appointments outside of answering questions about symptoms and such, and the atmosphere was always tense. He didn't try to make conversation with me on a personal level and only touched me to examine me. There was no "How do you like school?" or "What's your favorite color?" Only things like peering down my throat and "Say aaaaah." Once I was hospitalized for a very bad virus, and he brought me a robe as a gift. It was the only thing I ever received from him outside of the child support he was forced to pay.

When I was around 17, my father abruptly stopped seeing me as a patient because my mother said something to him that severed any type of contact. She asked him what would happen to me if something should ever happen to her. I suppose he didn't like the thought of that. He was still responsible for my medical bills, however, and his attorney mailed me a letter instructing me that I must pick up payment for such from the mailbox outside. I was not allowed to ever enter his office. Thus he heaped insult upon injury, and I never saw him again.

I never questioned my mother about my father. From my viewpoint he existed in a realm where it was impossible for me to go, even when he was physically right in front of me. Anything I have learned about him has been information she has volunteered. She told me that at the trial where she asked for more child support, he told the judge he couldn't afford to pay more, what with having to pay his gardener and such. He also balked at paying for my braces because he was paying for his stepdaughter's braces. The judge informed him that he might not have a moral obligation to his daughter, but he had a legal one, so the child support was raised and the orthodontic bill was paid.

After we married, Michael had the opportunity to meet my father once when he came to the clothing store where Michael worked. The owner, knowing the situation due to having known both my mother and father for years, made sure he introduced Michael to him. I am not sure if he made the connection as to who Michael was. Due to my mother's suggestion I'd sent him a wedding invitation but got no response. Michael told me his initial reaction upon finding out he was in the store was to feel like punching him, but when he saw that he was an old, frail man all he could think was how pitiful he looked.

Several years later, while I was driving around Brandon in the vicinity where he lived, it occurred to me that he must be getting very old and that he might die without ever having been saved. I assumed he hadn't repented of his sins because he'd never made any attempts at setting things right between us. My opinion was that if he had become a born-again believer at some point he would have tried to contact me and make amends. I thought to myself that if I could find out where he was living, I would send him a letter and in it explain the Gospel to him.

About a week later the most amazing thing happened. My mother by this time had married Gospel music songwriter Mosie Lister. They were looking for a condo in the vicinity of Brandon around a week after I'd had that thought. They were talking to the saleslady in the office of the first complex they visited and she was busily describing the amenities of the place. All of a sudden she offered up this information: "We have Dr. Hunter living here." My mother felt like she could have been knocked over with a feather. She didn't know about my earlier thought. She was just shocked he was living there and that the lady had volunteered the information.

After my mom arrived home, she called me to tell me what had happened. I told her I thought that was really bizarre, but I also realized that God was at work. Then I told her about the thought I'd had. The two of us set out to get his house number so I could follow through with my idea. The saleslady had unwittingly shown Mom and Mosie which unit was his, so we drove to his condo and I wrote the number down. When I got back home I sat down and composed my letter. In it I told him that I'd forgiven him for his actions and that I feared that when he died, *he* would be the one left without a Father. I also explained how he could know Jesus.

It surprised me when I got a reply from him, since I'd reached out to him before as a child by sending a letter and a drawing of a horse to him and got no response. In his letter he said he'd thought about contacting me before. He was self-righteous and defensive and proceeded to tell me I had no right to judge him, misapplying Matthew 7:1. There was no apology, no thanks for contacting him, no owning up to his wrong. He said he prayed the Lord's prayer for me and others every day (I don't really understand how you could pray that prayer for others; that really doesn't make any sense to me). I could not tell one way or the other by his response if he was saved, and I still had my doubts due to the nature of his reaction and his apparent lack of spiritual understanding. I was disappointed to say the least. Once again my father had failed in relating to me.

A couple years after Michael and I and our boys moved to Tennessee, my mother got word through the grapevine that my father was in Hospice. I knew then that his time was short and hoped he'd gotten saved. My mom had planned to visit and ended up being with us during the time his funeral was held. I looked at the obituary the Tampa Tribune posted online. My name was not mentioned, but my two half sisters and his wife and stepchildren were. "Par for the course", I thought. There was a section where people could post their comments. As I was scrolling through them, I came across one in which a woman had posted that she and her husband were glad to learn that he had accepted the Lord. Now, I do not know whether he had a deathbed conversion or if one happened some time before that. And I will never know the truth on this side of Heaven. Doubt still remains about him being born again, but for his sake I hope that what the woman said is true.

Over the years since his death, I've pondered the remarkable events that led to me being able to get in touch with my father. God acted, not when I prayed for Him to act, but when a thought crossed my mind. This has led me to believe that thought was intentionally placed there by God, especially since it seemed to come from out of the blue. Another thing I've wondered is whether God prompting me to send my father that letter was just as much for my peace of mind as it was to be a witness to him. God knew that if I found out my father died and I didn't have the chance to present the Gospel to him and offer forgiveness it would grow into a huge issue that would plague me for the rest of my life. In His sovereignty He initiated and arranged for that to become possible. I feel relieved that my father's blood is not on my hands, even if he did not accept the Lord, because I told him the Gospel message. I'm also relieved that I had the chance to verbalize forgiveness, regardless of how it was received. So you see, even though my earthly father couldn't have cared less about me or my feelings, my Heavenly Father sure did.

CHAPTER 6

OF HORSES AND MEN

*Delight yourself in the Lord and he will
give you the desires of your heart.*
—Psalm 37:4

Throughout my growing up years there were often
times of quiet despair. I don't remember ever
having any warm or affectionate feelings toward my
father during the time we had contact through the
doctor visits. I can't describe exactly how I felt then;
perhaps numb comes the closest. I think I was just
trying to make it through each appointment as it came,
since the whole situation seemed forced and, well—
weird. He was a total stranger to me who'd fathered
me, rather like a stray dog passing through the neigh-
borhood that manages to get through the fence to the
female. My mother may not view him or their relationship that way, but that's how it looks and feels from
my perspective. When he died, I didn't shed a single
tear, and I still haven't years later. I wasn't happy or

sad. How I felt and reacted mirrored exactly the treatment I'd received from him.

When I was little I was terrified of men. I was sure that they were going to cause me some kind of harm. If I saw a man in the toy store where I occasionally was allowed to go and browse in an aisle by myself, I would run to another aisle in an attempt to hide. As I grew older, the absence of male interaction along with my father's rejection lead me to believe that men were totally incapable of having feelings, much less getting them hurt. That has translated into lots of trouble in my marriage, because I felt like I could say anything to Michael and it wouldn't hurt him; after all, he was a man. It took several years for me to understand that wasn't the case.

I remember my mother dating a man to whom she became engaged when I was around six or seven. She says it was her attempt to find a father for me. He raced stock cars locally, and he had a daughter from a previous marriage. One time we had gone to watch him race, and I'd fallen asleep. He picked both me and his daughter up to carry us to the car, one on each shoulder, and I vaguely remember the warm feeling of being cared for by a father figure, and actually enjoying that experience. After that night I never felt it again. My mother ended up breaking off their relationship due to his unwillingness to attend church regularly.

As an adult I've had a couple of very unpleasant experiences with certain men who think that the child of an affair should remain cloaked in shame and the topic eschewed. This belief comes from those whose only difference from my parents was that they didn't get caught because nobody turned up pregnant. They judge with planks in their own eyes. My immediate reaction was anger, and following that, the same feelings of inferiority that plagued me since my youth. Words do wound, contrary to the old sticks and stones cliché. Then I began to think about the judging that was going on and that they were no better than I. We all sin, and each need God's grace. No one is any better than anyone else in God's estimation—we all "fall short of the glory of God." Sadly they neglected to take that into account, and further marred my view of the male gender to the point I had to take my own advice to heart and realize they were sinning, as we with sin still living in us do.

During the 70s, there was a TV show that aired every weekday called the *Monkees*.[2] It was originally produced from 1967-1968, and the reruns were a regular part of my afternoons. The show was about a band with four guys, a copy of the Beatles, with good looks and long hair. I liked the one named Davy Jones, the only Brit, boyishly handsome and possessing that wonderful accent. Recently I purchased two DVD sets of both seasons and as I was watching them, I could see why I was so attracted to him in particular. He was sweet, cute, and he was always trying to rescue the girl and get her out of impending danger or trouble. He didn't look like a man—he looked like a terribly handsome boy, so he was not threatening. He sang a song called "Daydream Believer"[3] and in it one of the lines mentions his being a white knight on a steed (icing on the cake, I loved horses and drew, drooled over, and read about them incessantly as a kid). What more could a young girl want? He set my heart dreaming about having that kind of male interaction in my life.

Only recently did I rediscover the *Monkees* because Michael, knowing I'd liked them, bought me a CD with some of their hits while he was at a truck stop out on the road. Then Christian came home with a vinyl album of theirs he'd gotten as a surprise for me from a vintage record shop in Nashville. These got me thinking that I'd like to see if Davy had a Facebook page to check up on him and see how he was. I found his web site and e-mailed whoever does his correspondence, just to say hi and that I'd grown up listening to Davy with the *Monkees*. I got a polite response from the person and they told me that Davy did have a Facebook page, which I promptly liked. On February 29, 2012, I saw a post on Facebook from one of my friends saying that Davy had passed away from a heart attack at the age of 66. I couldn't believe how sad I felt. After all, he was just some guy on TV. I didn't know him personally. While talking to Michael later about his death, I actually cried! It occurred to me that maybe the reason was that one of the few happy pieces of my childhood had disappeared with Davy.

After doing some research I found out that Davy had been in real life what he was on that small black and white TV screen, and he had been a horse lover as well! He and I even shared the same birthday. He appreciated his fans and went out of his way to show them. If he came across anyone in need he would help him or her out. I read story after story of his giving to others. And oddly enough, he began to remind me of someone else I know. Someone who had boyish good looks when we met, and who was kind and caring. Someone who sings professionally, goes out of his way for his fans, and helps people in need. If you haven't figured it out yet, I'm talking about Michael. Leave it to God to arrange for me to marry a man almost exactly like the one who inspired me as a young girl! Now where *is* that horse?

MICHAEL, HIS BROTHER, RONNIE, AND NEWCOMER PAUL
LANCASTER COMPRISE THE CURRENT BOOTH BROTHERS.

CHAPTER 7

RELATIONSHIPS

There's a song by artist John Mayer about the relationship between fathers and daughters. It addresses why fathers should be there in every way for them: because they grow up to become lovers and mothers, and their relationship with their father dictates how those future relationships will be affected.[4] The first time I heard it and read the lyrics it flew like an arrow deep into my soul. It made me feel like crying and shouting "Yes!" at the same time. I believe that, ultimately, in the lives of their daughters fathers represent God. I'm really thankful that this secular singer chose to record it because I hope that it will influence many young fathers who hear it.

As far as my own relationships go, where do I start? I feel as if I could be featured on some cable TV show for people whose insides are as messed up as a hoarder's home! There are things that need to be fixed, even though I haven't discovered what some of those things are because I can't see them or I'm in denial. There are deep piles of stuff I don't need but I keep hanging onto that hinder the kind of life I should and can have.

We had a foundation problem with our former home, and it affected more than just the area where the problem originated. It caused walls to crack and the kitchen cabinets to pull away. It illustrates what happens when the foundation isn't right—the problem travels to other areas of the home. The foundation of my life was so improperly laid that the whole thing has been affected by it. The areas of marriage, friendships, and parenthood have all been stressed and cracked by it.

I love my husband dearly but we've had some adjustments to make over the years and some valleys to traverse. At times I've taken my wrath and resentment against men out on him. When he fails to live up to my expectations, I see it as yet another failure of the male gender in relation to myself. And because of my father I have some pretty ridiculous expectations at times. I've had to work to understand that Michael's a good guy and that God wants to love me through him.

Sometimes I feel like we've had a relationship similar to Rhett Butler and Scarlett O'Hara. After their daughter, Bonnie, dies, a heartbroken Rhett tells Scarlett that he spoiled Bonnie rotten because it was his desire to do that for Scarlett, but she wouldn't let him.[5] I'm blessed because God gave me a husband who also wants to spoil me. He likes to take me out clothes shopping because he knows that I didn't have many clothes growing up. He tells me that sometimes he sees the little girl that I was and he feels badly about how I was treated and wants to try to make up for some of it. But one of the most difficult things for me to do is let him into my inner world. It causes intimacy to be difficult to achieve. I think the reluctance to open up to my spouse can be attributed to a trust issue that asks, "Can I really rely on you? Are you at some point going to reject me? Because I'm going to hedge against that." The rejection I fear doesn't have to be complete rejection, as in divorce; it could be a less severe form of rejection, such as simply not wanting to spend time with me.

In the area of friendships, having been abandoned has had the effect of me not trusting the unproven. I don't make friends easily; I build my walls strong and high. I expect to try people for a while before admitting them into my confidence, and if any hint of trouble starts to emerge I will write that person off before I end up being the object of rejection yet again. This is built into my thinking and the possibility of it happening is always subconsciously there. That is why I prefer my old friends to new ones. Time has proven them, and I know what to expect. If they haven't deserted me after this long, I trust that they won't.

Being a mother to my children has been the easiest of my relationships. I was blessed to have a mother who took good care of me, and that has translated into me trying to do my best for my kids. When each tiny person came into the world and needed to be cared for, those mothering instincts just kicked in automatically. That's not to say I don't have my struggles and days where I want to change my name to something else besides Mom, however! Nor is it to say that I haven't done some bad parenting and risked alienating my kids. I try to admit when I'm wrong, apologize and ask for forgiveness, however.

Having my own children has had the effect of making it more difficult to understand how any parent could abandon their child. There are days that are extremely frustrating when I want to be anywhere but in my parenting role. But I've never wanted to leave them permanently. I suppose the effects of my rejection show up at times when they've disappointed me with bad behavior and I feel myself pulling away emotionally. That's when I have to remind myself to act out love for them as a choice. After any punishment I always hug and reassure them that I love them, and that I have their best interests at heart. I never want them to feel the parental rejection I felt.

I keep reminding myself that life is a process. I also know that the only time our relating will be perfected is when we stand in God's presence, with our sinful nature finally conquered. In the meantime, God continually reveals where I go wrong in His efforts at sanctification. I'm thankful that in His sight, through Christ, I have already achieved that goal even if it isn't reality for me yet: "...because by one sacrifice He has made perfect forever those who are being made holy."—Hebrews 10:14

CHAPTER 8

THE CURE

Therefore put on the full armor of
God, so that when the day of evil
comes, you may be able to stand
your ground, and after you have done
everything, to stand. Stand firm then,
with the belt of truth buckled around
your waist, with the breastplate of
righteousness in place, and with your
feet fitted with the readiness that
comes from the gospel of peace. In
addition to all this, take up the shield
of faith, with which you can extin-
guish all the flaming arrows of the evil
one. Take the helmet of salvation and
**the sword of the Spirit, which is the
word of God**. —Ephesians 6:13-17

Depression has been an ugly issue at various times over the course of my life. I have a

melancholy personality, but sometimes it becomes magnified. Considering my family's history of addiction, OCD, and moodiness, it is easy to understand why, when you mix in the rejection, you have a recipe for depression. This has lead to some very destructive ways of thinking and feeling at different points, especially when stress seemed to be at its worst.

There were times when I got so depressed in the years after I was married that I began having suicidal thoughts. I felt like a failure as a wife and a mother; I was very ill equipped for the situations I faced, having come from a dysfunctional family where normal was not taught or observable. I thought that my husband and oldest son would be better off without me and my inability to be positive, and speculated that Michael would be happier with someone more upbeat. Feeling that I couldn't do anything right was just an argument away. Michael didn't know how to respond when I expressed those thoughts and feelings. When he was traveling and I tearfully told him what I was thinking during our phone conversations he would become silent. He just didn't know what to say or do and wasn't equipped to help.

When the Booth Brothers' schedule was extremely heavy when we lived in Florida and the group was being built, I began having anxiety and panic attacks. Once, after some surgery I'd had, I looked to see what Michael's schedule was going to be like. When I saw how many dates were booked, I lost it. Michael had to come off the road for that weekend (the only time he's ever altered his schedule as a result of any of my personal issues). The breaking point came because there was no end in sight to the traveling and I was in pain, struggling to recover from the surgery. Thankfully I was able to get it together after that weekend, but I still struggled with anxiety from time to time.

I tried medications but couldn't deal with their side effects. There were times when I would think through different methods of suicide, but the one thing that always kept me from getting more serious about it was my middle son, Jonathan. Jonathan was literally my lifesaver on more than one occasion. He needed me and I knew it. He was a mama's boy. I knew I couldn't just abandon him. I couldn't stand the thought of him being reared by someone else who might not understand him or care about him the way I did.

I found myself in the depths of one of my depression episodes when my oldest son was in first grade. I was homeschooling him and taking care of a toddler and it wasn't going well at all. He and I were butting heads because he didn't want to do his work, so at that point we decided to enroll him in a Christian school. When my friend found out that I was going to be freed up from homeschooling, she invited me to come to the Bible study she was attending. I halfheartedly agreed.

I showed up to the introduction class slightly on edge. My friend had explained the aspects of it, and it sounded a little hard and nothing like what I'd ever experienced; if you missed over three weeks in a row they kicked you out! Still a little unsure about the whole thing, I listened to the lecture that day and the lady speaking was excellent. Judging by the way she presented the lesson, I decided this was something I wanted to do.

Placement in this Bible study isn't always immediate. Sometimes there is a waiting list, but I was placed right away. I eagerly attended the small group times and the lectures and practically inhaled the notes and did my homework. I made sure I arrived on time because I didn't want to get locked out of my small group (they would lock you out if you were over ten minutes late!) One day I realized that I was no longer depressed and that the cure for my depression had come in the form of studying God's word. I'm not talking about just reading God's word; I'm talking about getting in there and digging out answers to what were sometimes very difficult questions.

It was no coincidence that my friend invited me to this study, nor that they were in the middle of the book of John. This was a divine appointment. Even though they systematically study entire books of the Bible for a year instead of covering topics, it was exactly what I needed to address the problems I was having. It was like a healing balm to my wounded spirit.

Before I joined my Bible study, I couldn't understand why I didn't have much power to deal with temptations that crouched at my door. Sitting in church listening to sermons had not accomplished much more than making me frustrated for many years, since I was convicted of sin but didn't quite know how to deal with my huge issues. Various people stressed having a quiet time, but I was never successful at implementing one. Occasionally I tried reading the Bible without much success at being able to decipher its finer theological points or seeing how it fit together as a whole, rather like a toddler with a thousand-piece jigsaw puzzle.

Looking back it seems I must have been expecting God to somehow impart knowledge to me without me having to do the hard work of reading, pondering, and facing my own shortcomings, which is now required of me via formal study. I am convinced that sound doctrine and theology are the keys to human happiness. First we must know who Christ is and what His standing is. Then, we need to know where we stand with God in Christ. This will conquer our fears. One of the best books for studying this and probably tied with John for my favorite book is Hebrews.

Only as we act in faith on God's truth already written in the scriptures will He reveal more of Himself to us. John 14:23 says, "Jesus replied, 'If anyone loves Me, he will obey My teaching. My Father will love him, and We will come to him and make Our home with him.' " Matthew 5:8 says, "Blessed are the pure in heart, for they will see God." The first step is to believe and receive salvation. If you are not born again you do not have the Holy Spirit to help you understand the Bible and it will be foolishness to you (1 Corinthians 2:14). The next is to get into the word and study it diligently, craving pure spiritual milk (1 Peter 2:2). In this way we are to grow up in our salvation.

For someone who struggles with depression I highly recommend finding a good Bible study that teaches sound doctrine. It will transform your mind and life. You must get to know Who God is in order to deal with yourself and any issues you have. Getting to know Him is accomplished through studying the Bible. The more you focus on Him and His character, the less chance you have for all kinds of mental ills befalling you, and if they find occasion to you will have a weapon with which to fight back.

Depression still lurks in the shadowy areas of my life, but when it finds opportunity, coils itself around me and starts to constrict I know how to extract myself, and I know that it won't last forever. Whenever I have episodes I picture myself in the bottom of a deep hole. Then I mentally force myself to go over to that hole, throw myself a rope, and pull myself up out of it.

Immersing myself in God's word or theology books, anything to learn more or be reminded about God and His character helps, as does refocusing myself on what I can do to help others. From my experience battling depression is a process that must be repeated, but once you've found the cure it becomes less difficult. One day I and other believers who experience it won't have to deal with it anymore, and what a day that will be! "And I heard a loud voice from the throne saying, 'Now the dwelling of God is with men, and He will live with them. They will be His people, and God Himself will be with them and be their God. He will wipe every tear from their eyes. There will be no more death or mourning or crying or pain, for the old order of things has passed away.' "— Revelation 21:3,4

CHAPTER 9

GOD'S CHARACTER

Gradually I have come to understand that when we go through trials we must stake everything on God's character. That's the only way we can have peace in the midst of any crisis. For some reason God has allowed me to experience quite a bit of pain lately. After some testing in conjunction with reviewing my symptoms, my doctor believes I have contracted Lyme disease and my immune system could possibly be reacting to it. Some days the pain can be debilitating. Why is the Lord allowing it? My guess is that it is for refining my own character to become more like that of Christ, and to slow me down enough to draw me closer to Him.

Do I believe God can heal me? Absolutely. I have asked, even begged tearfully on more than one occasion. My reaction to this trial has been different than my reaction to others. I am trusting in God's character more, because since previous trials I've studied and discovered more about His character. My prayer is that I will learn what it is He wants me to learn through this experience, and that He will receive all the glory for the outcome.

Had I understood God's character better during my youth it would have saved me a lot of heartache. The Church taught me that God loves, John 3:16 style. For some reason it never sank in that God wanted a real relationship with me. I thought I was supposed to keep His rules so I'd remain in good standing, not out of gratitude for my salvation. I was also under the impression that whenever I messed up, He was going to angrily punish me. As a teenager I lived under constant pressure, feeling that God was completely unhappy with me, which was in large part due to my lifestyle. I thought His unhappiness stemmed from His anger at me, not that my sinning was causing broken fellowship with Him. I believe I was saved as a youngster; therefore, the condemnation I felt was completely manufactured, either by the enemy or my own mind. Scripture says "Therefore, there is now no condemnation for those who are in Christ Jesus, because through Christ Jesus the law of the Spirit of life set me free from the law of sin and death"—Romans 8:1. Once we are born again, we are clothed with Christ (Galatians 3:27). God sees us as He sees Christ, as if we'd never sinned. All that we do in keeping God's commands should be out of thankfulness for God's amazing act of being declared innocent before Him.

What I should have been feeling was conviction. Conviction makes us sad for our actions against God and makes us want to right our wrongs. The Bible says Godly sorrow brings repentance (2 Corinthians 7:10). But somewhere along the line, because of my messed up view of God, that conviction was overshadowed by condemnation. Satan sold me the same lie he sold to Eve in the Garden, which was that God really doesn't have your best interest at heart. I lived under a mistaken perception of what God is really like for most of my life. It wasn't until I started taking getting to know

God seriously that it changed. God worked in spite of my feelings of condemnation and brought me out of that dark place. He worked until I realized that my object of affection should be Him.

God's character and attributes are wonderful for the believer to behold and meditate upon. The more I study it the more I am amazed. God is sovereign; His plans cannot be thwarted: "When this happens, you will know that I am the Sovereign Lord."—Ezekiel 24:24. He is unchanging, the same today, yesterday and forever: "But You remain the same, and your years will never end."—Psalm 102:27. He is trustworthy: "Anyone who trusts in Him will never be put to shame" —Romans 10:11. He keeps His promises and covenants for His name's sake—David said in Psalm 145:13 "The Lord is faithful to all His promises..." and in Psalm 143:11 said, "For your name's sake, O Lord, preserve my life." He is loving: "You, O God, are my fortress, my loving God."—Psalm 59:17. He is the Good Shepherd and He leads the righteous; according to Isaiah 40:11, "He tends His flock like a shepherd: He gathers the lambs in His arms and carries them close to His heart; He gently leads those who have young." God is unique: "I am God and there is no other; I am God, and there is none like me."—Isaiah 46:9. The Lord is omniscient: "I make known the end from the beginning, from ancient times what is still to come." –Isaiah 46:10. God is just: "The works of His hands are faithful and just."—Psalm 111:7. He is righteous: "The Lord is righteous in all His ways."—Psalm 145:17. He is omnipotent and wise: "He made the earth by His power; He founded the world by His wisdom and stretched out the heavens by His understanding."—Jeremiah 51:15. And this isn't even a complete list!

Is Jesus the same as the Father in His character and attributes? Absolutely! Hebrews 1:3 says, "The Son is the radiance of God's glory and the exact representation of His being, sustaining all things by His powerful word." John 1:1 says, "In the beginning was the Word, and the Word was with God, and the Word was God. He was with God in the beginning. Through Him all things were made; without Him nothing was made that has been made." In John 14:8, Philip requested that Jesus show the disciples the Father. Jesus answered, "Don't you know Me, Philip, even after I have been among you such a long time? Anyone who has seen Me has seen the Father."

Given all these truths about God, how will I not trust Him to know what is best for me, and to understand that it is He who is ultimately in control of my life? I've no reason to live in fear anymore, so I've begun to combat fearful thoughts when they arise. The enemy cannot do anything to a believer unless God allows it, and God is the only one who can do anything about our circumstances. God may not change our circumstances, but He has promised to be with us *through* them. He was with Abraham, Isaac, Jacob, Joseph, Moses, Joshua, and countless others, and He has likewise promised Christians that He will never leave us or forsake us. Jesus was separated from God on the cross so that we would never have to endure that separation ourselves.

CHAPTER 10

GOD AS FATHER

A father to the fatherless, a defender of
widows, is God in His holy dwelling.
—Psalm 68:5

I've struggled all my life with seeing God as a father, in spite of the many scriptures that say that's the relationship He has with believers. When praying I almost always call Him Lord. Only recently have I occasionally addressed Him as Father. After studying Islam a bit I realized my concept of God over the years has more closely resembled the Islamic one that says their god is a distant, unknowable being—and why wouldn't it be since my father was distant and unknowable? The Bible contradicts this in many places with verses about believers being considered sons, praying, "Our Father", calling God "Abba, Father", etc. but those terms have been very difficult to accept and believe. Not having a healthy relationship with my biological father has greatly hindered my relationship with God, as has my own human rebellion against Him.

One of the hardest things I've had to overcome over the years is anger toward God since He is sovereign. Certainly God could have kept my situation from happening. He could have given me to married parents. He could have prevented the pregnancy. He could have done any number of things to spare me the hardship, but He didn't. I do not believe He allowed my mother to become pregnant as a punishment, as some would conclude. Jesus was already punished for her sin (all of it) when He died on the cross. The question "Why?" has come up at many points throughout the years. Here are a few of what I think are some answers:

- God has used it and is using it in refining me to make me more like Jesus.
- God has used it and is using it to prepare me for something.
- God is using it to enable me to be more compassionate to those who struggle or suffer.
- God allows us to choose to sin or not, and our choices affect those around us.
- God used rejection for my protection.

Another difficulty has been believing that God would initiate a relationship with me based on unconditional love. I understand that most girls normally experience love from their dads that doesn't have to be earned, which simulates God's love. That kind of male love ended for me when my grandfather died. The dating and marrying experiences require a give and take kind of love so they did nothing to repair my broken concept. God has patiently worked on me in this respect through studying His word, however.

In recent years I've gotten to know, through Bible study, more of what God is truly like. I believe the best picture we have of God and His personality and character is found in the person of Jesus. One of my very favorite verses is Hebrews 1:3: "The Son is the radiance of God's glory and the exact representation of His being." The disciple Philip asked Jesus to show them the Father, and Jesus' response to him was that if you have seen Him, you have seen the Father (John 14:9). So I can study the person of Christ to find out how God feels about and relates to His children.

I have also learned to fight lies with scripture. I've had to ignore what my mind tells me God is like and believe what the Bible tells me He is like and how He looks at believers. The Word is truth, and it's the only way I can discover God's true attributes. When my aunt was terminally ill, I questioned, "Why is God letting my aunt die from breast cancer?" This translates into "Doesn't He care?" The Holy Spirit immediately brought to my remembrance scripture which answered, "Precious in the sight of the Lord is the death of His saints."—Psalm 116:15. God was looking forward to the time when my aunt would be able to greet Him face to face and be delivered from her affliction and this sin-cursed world. My mind on occasion taunts me with, "You are worthless, you can't do anything right". The Word says I was worth the death of God's Son: "For God so loved the world that He gave His one and only Son, that whoever believes in Him shall not perish but have eternal life."–John 3:16. My mind sometimes belittles me by saying, "You're illegitimate, a mistake. You shouldn't have been born." The Bible says, "All the days ordained for me were written in your book before one of them came to be."—Psalm 139:16. This is what scripture is referring to when it exhorts us to be transformed by the renewing of our minds.

The Bible says God takes it upon Himself to be a Helper of and Father to the fatherless. A couple of verses where this is made clear are: "You are the helper of the fatherless"—Psalm 10:14; "A Father to the fatherless, a defender of widows, is God in His holy dwelling"—Psalm 68:5. As I continue to grow in the knowledge of Christ I gradually feel more like I can trust God as a Father who wants what is best for me. I am still a work in progress, and the promise I have is this: "Being confident of this, that He who began a good work in you will carry it on to completion until the day of Christ Jesus."—Philippians 1:6.

CHAPTER 11

WHAT AM I WORTH?

Surely He took up our infirmities and carried our sorrows, yet we considered Him stricken by God, smitten by Him, and afflicted.. But He was pierced for our transgressions, He was crushed for our iniquities; the punishment that brought us peace was upon Him; and by His wounds we are healed.
—Isaiah 53:4,5

Recently I came across a plastic storage bin containing all sorts of awards I'd garnered as a young person. Starting at the age of nine and continuing through college I entered art competitions and managed to win or place in many—most years I won some sort of award. I also earned academic awards, band awards and medals, citizenship awards, and leadership awards. My grades allowed me to become a member of the National Honor Society. Becoming a Hillsborough County and Tampa Tribune Honor Student lead to being awarded a scholarship to the University of Tampa. I was extremely competitive and wanted to be the best at everything, and managed to do very well except when I entered beauty pageants—oh yes, I did a couple of those too!

As I was showing these to Michael (believe it or not he'd never seen most of them in almost 20 years of marriage), it dawned on me that all my growing up years I'd been driven to prove my worthiness. Somehow I had to show others that in spite of my dubious origins, I deserved to be here and to be liked and respected. If I could be the best, then I would be worth people's time and attention. I wasn't an outgoing person; I could not rely on my personality to endear myself to others, so I tried to use my talent. I always wanted to be better than the next guy so that I could feel superior in some fashion, because I certainly wasn't in regards to background. The only problem with this approach is that it did nothing to build lasting relationships. Oh, I got attention for the short while that I was in the spotlight. But then it was gone and I'd have to win again to get more recognition. Looking back it seems it almost operated like an addiction.

Like me you may have trouble comprehending how much we are worth to God. A few years ago I had it illustrated for me. The person who was counseling me drew a scale like the ones that have to have the same amount of weight on each side for them to balance. On one side of the scale, he drew a diamond. Then he described a scenario about finding a diamond, taking it to be appraised, and discovering it was worth $10,000. He wrote this amount on the other side of the scale. In order to purchase the diamond, someone would have to be willing to pay $10,000. Then he erased the diamond and the $10,000. He drew a stick figure on one side of the scale. Then he asked me, "How much was God willing to pay for you?" As the question began to penetrate my mind, I came to the realization that God was willing to pay with the agonizing death of His only Son. Huge tears started running down my cheeks. I didn't answer; he saw that I knew.

We aren't worth something because we possess some inherent good qualities, because we don't. We aren't worth something because of our talents, our personality, our social status, our family, or our wealth. We are worth the death of God's Son because God thinks so. Jesus was perfect and kept the requirements of God's law that were impossible for us to keep (Hebrews 4:15). He paid the price and endured God's wrath against our sin in our place (Isaiah 53:4-6). God and Jesus both thought we were worth it. "But God demonstrates his own love for us in this: While we were still sinners, Christ died for us."—Romans 5:8. He did it because He loves us in spite of our absolutely dismal performance.

CHAPTER 12

VICTORY OVER VICTIMHOOD

There are those in this life who've
been dealt a poor hand,
But they've overcome and by God's strength they stand
Those who have come through unbearable loss
Not defined by the past but defined by the Cross[6]

It's very easy to fall into the trap of believing we are victims, especially when voices from all directions tell us that we've been wronged and we deserve compensation or to be excused from our actions. Just think about all the ads on TV for attorneys soliciting all sorts of lawsuits. You spilled hot coffee in your lap? Sue the place from which you purchased it, they should have warned you it was hot! Committed a crime while you were on prescription drugs? It's not your fault; it's the fault of the drugs you were taking. Because of this I have found some very amusing and at the same time sad warning labels on many of the products I purchase. Apparently quite a few folks do not want to take responsibility for their actions these days and are looking for someone to blame.

If anyone had reason to claim being a victim and lay blame, Joseph did. Thrown into a pit, almost murdered, and finally sold into slavery at the age of 17 by his jealous brothers, he was carted off to Egypt and purchased by Potiphar, Pharaoh's Captain of the Guard. He was tempted to commit adultery with Potiphar's wife, and when he refused, she framed him and he was thrown into prison. Then, after giving God's interpretation of the dreams of two fellow prisoners who were Pharaoh's household servants, he was forgotten by one of them after the man was restored to his former position as Pharaoh's cupbearer. Two years went by before the cupbearer remembered to mention Joseph to Pharaoh (after Pharaoh had some troubling dreams of his own). However, Joseph never blamed anyone for his lot in life. Instead, he persevered, acknowledged the sovereignty of God in his circumstances, and treated those who'd mistreated him with compassion. The Bible makes it very clear that even though Joseph was wronged on many levels, God was always with him and he was favored because of God's presence, eventually becoming second only to Pharaoh.

In stark contrast to Joseph's reactions to being treated unfairly, I've played the victim many times by blaming my mistakes and shortcomings on my dysfunctional upbringing. But as long as I keep buying into this mentality it keeps me bound. It is almost impossible to grow spiritually and emotionally as long as I think I'm owed something by someone for some perceived wrong, or that I'm not responsible for my actions. As long as I am self-focused, which is what happens when one believes they are a victim, I cannot see God. My eyes are not on Him because they are on me. Then my spiritual life stagnates.

What I've had to learn over the years (and I'm still learning) is that I need to take responsibility for my actions, regardless of whether or not they are the result of something that happened to me in the past. For me it's a choice with which I'm faced on a pretty regular basis. I recently heard a sermon on the Prodigal Son where the preacher made this statement: "God is sovereign. We become spiritually mature when we stop blaming our parents." How hard that is, especially when you've suffered some real wrongs at a parent's hands! However, God gives us the opportunity to make choices, and I have His word to assist me in that; therefore I have no excuse. If I choose properly, there is victory rather than victimhood. Proverbs 2:6-8: "For the Lord gives wisdom, and from his mouth come knowledge and understanding. He holds victory in store for the upright, He is a shield to those whose walk is blameless For He guards the course of the just and protects the way of His faithful ones." We must repent for our own rebellion against God and must make up our minds to become overcomers rather than victims. We need to take the words of the song to heart and not let our pasts define us, but be defined by the cross.

CHAPTER 13

FATHER'S DAY, OR NOT

*One man considers one day more
sacred than another; another man
considers every day alike. Each one
should be fully convinced in his own
mind. —Romans 14:5*

I sometimes dislike assembling with the Church on Father's Day, and regrettably for me whoever invented it ensured that it falls on a Sunday every year. Michael is almost always traveling so I have to go by myself. I'd rather not listen to the usual sermon on fatherhood loaded with advice on how to be a good one and pats on the back for those who are. It brings up every area in which my own father failed, which covers pretty much every area. Another thing that makes me extremely uncomfortable is that I feel like I have to wish every father I see a Happy Father's Day. Sometimes I feel the urge welling up inside to yell, "I hate Father's Day, it stinks!"

Some years I give myself permission to not go to church on Father's Day and not feel guilty about it. My mother never placed an undue emphasis on church attendance. She was and still is a person who understands that our relationship to God doesn't depend on how many times per week we meet in a church building. Meetings on Sunday mornings, Sunday evenings, and Wednesday nights are manmade traditions. Relating to and drawing strength from other believers can be done in many ways, at different times, and in various places, especially since the invention of the internet. Worship of God can take place right inside my home, and in my case is more apt to be true worship versus the kind that goes on in front of other people. I'm not saying to forsake meeting with other believers in an official capacity because scripture teaches otherwise, but if there are certain days in which it is difficult to physically be around other people then I believe it's okay to arrange your day to accommodate that.

Having said that, there are years where I have forced myself to go to church and received a blessing for being there that day. I sit and struggle to perceive God as not being up there aloof and distant; I wrestle with the idea of Him functioning as a Father. Sometimes I succeed at getting the message He intends. And that message is that He is unlike my biological father in every respect. I have to maintain a very different picture of what God is like. Only scripture can accurately inform that picture. But no matter where I am, God is not angry with me for whichever choice I've made, whether to be in church or out. I've received blessings from Him regardless of where I've chosen to be on that day.

CHAPTER 14

VENGEANCE

"It is mine to avenge; I will repay."
—*Deuteronomy 32:35*

Over the years opportunities for vengeance against my father have occasionally arisen. The first came when one of my half sisters (whom I met for the first time when I was 22) confided that he was an alcoholic while he was still practicing medicine. She admonished me not to tell anyone for fear he would lose his practice. During the time in which he was still working, I never told anyone. I could have used that opportunity to ruin him.

Another arose when he died. It was very difficult reading the glowing remarks people of the community had posted about him in his online obituary considering, in my experience, he wasn't the marvelous person they portrayed. I could have exposed him publicly for what I felt he truly was, sullied his reputation, and in the process dealt an awful lot of pain to his grieving stepfamily, particularly his stepdaughter. Apparently the two of them had a very close bond, judging from what she wrote in her tribute to him and from what my mother had learned from one of his close associates. Her words were extremely hard for me to process, because he had essentially denied his own flesh and blood daughter, me, in favor of her, a stranger's daughter. All those times I had longed for my father to care about me, he was too busy caring about someone totally unrelated to him biologically. Seeing her refer to him as "Daddy" was particularly painful. Therefore, I had to exercise a ton of restraint and resist posting something derogatory about him, which would have laid bare what I knew about him for everyone to see. Battling my emotions, I fought with myself for days. I kept telling myself that the right was not mine, and that God claims all rights to vengeance on behalf of His children.

A couple of my relatives thought I should contest my father's will. I decided that I would refrain from doing so. I told my mother that I would wait for God's justice regarding my father's estate, and, in the end, never received anything of his. However, I know God has something better in mind. As His daughter, I already possess an inheritance that will not fade nor perish. The Bible instructs us to lay up treasure in Heaven, not on the earth. Anything I could have received from him wouldn't last anyway, and may have actually served to harm in some way. My rest came from belief in God's sovereignty and care.

Recently someone mailed my mother the obituary of my father's last wife. She passed away at the age of 70. She too had an online obituary. Another opportunity for evil presented itself, and again the battle raged. I was tempted to write something mean in order to get back at her daughter. Again I refrained. I have a feeling that my father's stepdaughter doesn't know my own dear, true, heavenly Father, nor does He know her. And that shall be to her a bigger loss by far than what I ever suffered from not knowing the man she called Daddy.

Please understand that I'm not writing about my temptations for retribution and how I responded to them in order to make myself look good. I'm relating them to show that we are all tempted to take revenge, and that it is possible, even in the face of great injustice, to not act on it. I am also not saying I didn't sin in my attitudes, because I am quite sure that I did during these times. I'm just really happy I didn't act out and hurt anyone, and that being God's child gives me the option to not act on temptation.

Peace has come from leaving the payback department up to God when it comes to my father. He claims it for Himself, and He can do a far better job of avenging His children than anyone else. I believe He doesn't want us burdened down with what vengeance produces in our hearts. He tells us to forgive, and He will confront our adversaries and those who wrong us. How God chose to deal with the situation on my behalf remains shrouded in mystery; perhaps it is better to not know. What is certain is that He did deal with my father in some way, because as He says in His word, "I will repay."

CHAPTER 15

A DILEMMA

Religion that God our Father accepts as
pure and faultless is this: to look after
orphans and widows in their distress...
—James 1:27

When I was growing up the men in the church were kind to me from a distance. They might have something cute or amusing to say but that was about the extent of it. My fifth grade teacher was a friend of my mom and she and her husband, who were believers, always bought me a few small gifts at Christmas. My uncle and aunt always attended my band concerts. I mentioned earlier the dad of the guy I dated who took the time to pay me attention. But there was nothing official in the churches of which I was a member to deal with kids or teenagers without dads. I wish that somewhere someone could come up with an answer as to how to minister to this expanding group. I am disappointed with the church's lack of attention to fatherless children. No church with which I've been involved has a ministry specifically for them; perhaps somewhere there exists such a ministry of which I'm unaware. I realize that it would be a difficult thing to implement and will admit that I don't have all the answers.

One of the difficulties in serving these children is that you cannot have married men become a father figure to fatherless kids without the involvement of their wives. It would not be prudent for the obvious reason that an attachment could form between the child's mother and the man, which could lead to them having an affair. And even if the wife was involved, there is still an element of risk. I'm convinced many women who are married would not want their husband paying a lot of attention to the child of a single mother. It may be hypocritical of me but I wouldn't want my own husband doing that—maybe more so than others because I have never had a father-daughter relationship, which makes me very jealous for my husband's attention. I am still a work in progress in some areas regarding my past!

Another difficulty is that in today's world there seem to be so many accusations of child molestation as well as actual occurrences of it. Some men might be afraid of being accused and some mothers might be afraid their child could become a victim. As you can see this is a complex issue and in my opinion anyone who chose to take it on would have to have a special calling to do so, as well as a lot of accountability.

I just finished an interesting book about marriage in which the author, the pastor of a church, encourages the single men of his church to consider the single mothers in the congregation when looking for someone to date. He states that single moms need husbands and their kids need fathers. He uses the passage in 1 Timothy Chapter 5 about widows to support his case.[7] I think this is a plausible solution for some and I wish more pastors would examine it in regards to their own churches and singles.

This generation is the most fatherless one to date. With more and more children being born out of wedlock I would love to see the church come up with a special way of ministering to these hurting people. They need to know that there is help, hope and that in spite of their origins God loves them. It would be wonderful if God raised up a ministry dedicated to them.

CHAPTER 16

AN IMPASSIONED PLEA

*His divine power has given us every-
thing we need for life and godliness
through our knowledge of Him who
called us by His own glory and good-
ness. Through these He has given us
His very great and precious promises,
so that through them you may partic-
ipate in the divine nature and escape
the corruption in the world caused by
evil desires. —2 Peter 1:3,4*

As I am writing this, there are riots in London,
with unruly, dangerous youths roaming the
streets, violently taking what does not belong to
them, destroying property and harming or even killing
people in the process. Today I read an internet article
explaining the reasons why this is happening: the
socialist government in Great Britain has for the past
30 or so years pushed an evil agenda on the poor of

that nation. The lies that poverty stricken women have bought into are that they don't need men and that it's acceptable to have sex outside of wedlock. Such behavior has been enabled with government entitlements. So transient men have sexual relations with these women and walk out of their and the resulting children's lives, never to bear any responsibility for them. Then the children grow up angry and maladjusted due to not having a strong father figure in the home. Basically all this bad behavior is the result of the breakdown of the family structure.[8]

You may be wondering why I'm writing about the issues affecting another country. It's because this example provides a good illustration of the effects of widespread fatherlessness regardless of the country in which it occurs. What follows is a plea from someone who has lived through being a fatherless child. It is designed in hopes that it will help whoever reads it to resist the temptation to have sex outside marriage, and to describe what happens to children who are conceived and born in this manner.

Whereas when I was a child being born out of wedlock was something of which to be ashamed, today it has become acceptable, almost expected within some groups of people in the United States. Currently, 40.8% of babies are born to unmarried parents.[9] Many single girls and women are no longer ashamed if they become pregnant, but are instead enabled and celebrated. It's even being glorified on television shows. This only encourages more of the same. Satan has sold people the lie that illicit sex and illegitimacy are okay. We need to take a sober look at how this is affecting our nation and not only it but also the lives of individuals.

This is a warning to those choosing to have sexual relations outside the confines of marriage. If they heed it they will save themselves a lot of heartache. Please don't misunderstand; I appreciate women and girls who decide to have their babies whenever they become pregnant while unmarried, just as I appreciate my own mother for doing so. In no way do I endorse aborting an unexpected child. For those who feel they cannot care for a child, adoption is what I consider the only option. But having sex outside of wedlock is sin, plainly put. Since the Bible has always held it to be so I'll not sugarcoat it. Just as when Eve and then Adam broke God's law, shame is the result of sin. There were no other people before whom they were ashamed—it was because of them realizing that God knew exactly what they had done. This was about their relationship with Him. There is shame in having sex outside marriage. There is shame in becoming pregnant without a husband. Shame is the result of the violation of God's law and the broken relationship with God Himself.

Participation in an illicit affair affects not only the mother but the baby, who is innocent of any wrongdoing. The stigma attached to being illegitimate still exists in the heart of the child, regardless of what society has allowed to become acceptable. As I have pointed out before, God's laws are written on our hearts. Then there are people who still believe, and rightly so, that an illegitimate baby is the result of sinful behavior, but they treat the mother or child or both with contempt, as if they themselves had never broken any of God's laws. All this wounding that occurs sets a child up for a lot of failure throughout life and especially if they never come to Jesus for healing.

Beyond the stigma there is also the deep down rejection that the child feels. Often their reality is that they are not loved by one of the people who helped bring about their existence. They see other children with loving fathers and wonder what is so wrong with them that it would cause their father to want nothing to do with them. Much of the child's life will be spent dealing with rejection, anger, resentment and how to forgive their parents. These will ultimately spill over into all the relationships they form, including marriage, and will haunt them for life unless they allow God to teach them how to overcome them. This rejection also explains why kids without dads get themselves into all kinds of trouble. It's been well documented that children without fathers are prone to all kinds of risky behavior, from doing drugs and drinking to having illicit sex and more.

Equally as destructive as the rejection and resulting negative emotions is the absence of the father in the home. No mother can make up for the missing father. Fathers provide a balance to the feminine. They bring masculinity, leadership, strength, provision, and protection to the equation. Without the father's example the child doesn't see correct male behavior or a committed relationship modeled. They are deprived of seeing the fullness of God's image (Genesis 1:27) and they will struggle in how to relate to Him as their Heavenly Father. Those who engage in sex outside marriage need to look beyond themselves and realize that their actions could produce another life, and anything less than God's design is not good enough.

Fatherless children are more often than not raised in poverty. My mother and I lived under the poverty level until I was a young adult, and we did not accept government assistance. At Thanksgiving one year, when I was too young to be able to tell the difference, she bought a chicken and passed it off as a turkey. One Christmas she didn't have money for gifts, so she made them. My clothes and shoes were newly purchased at the beginning of every school year and they had to last me all year. I went for long periods without haircuts. We needed a new refrigerator once and she had to borrow money from her boss to purchase it. Air conditioning was a luxury we couldn't afford until I was about 16, and Florida is a really hot, humid place without it. I didn't go off with my friends on weekends when I was in middle and high school and I certainly didn't get an allowance. I'm sure the financial burden was very difficult for my mom to endure.

Here are some statistics from the Heritage Foundation: "In America, children raised in a home with their biological mother and father are 82 percent less likely to be poor. The U.S. Department of Health finds 63 percent of youth suicides are from fatherless homes. Seventy-one percent of all high school dropouts come from fatherless homes, according to the National Principals Associations. And the National Fatherhood Initiative finds the absence of a biological father increases by 900 percent a daughter's vulnerability to rape and sexual abuse."[10]

My hope for women is that they will decide not to fulfill sinful sexual desires. The time for choice is before the bed is made. From one time of pleasure can come a lifetime of hardship. They should consider the hardships, not the time of emotional, sensual gratification. The hardships far outweigh the pleasure. Thinking about all the consequences I've mentioned and imagining saddling a child with them should give anyone pause. The decision to have sex without being married is a self-centered, self-gratifying one. Often men are portrayed in a bad light and the girl/woman is portrayed as the victim, but let's get real for a moment here. Men sometimes use women for sex, but women sometimes use men for emotional gratification. Women can be skilled manipulators. The entire fifth chapter of Proverbs and chapter six, verses 20-29 attest to this. Here's just a portion:

> To keep you from the evil woman,
> From the flattering tongue of a seductress.
> Do not lust after her in your heart,
> Nor let her allure you with the beauty of her eyelids. (NKJV)

I confess that as a teenager I was sometimes guilty of this type of conduct. Women can become enamored with wielding such power over men, and I was not immune. Unfortunately not many men can withstand it, especially if they do not know God. My reason for acting in such a manner and always having to have a boyfriend came from the lack of wholesome male involvement in my life. Still it does not make such behavior right. Thankfully God did not allow me to end up in the same situation as my mother although there was plenty of opportunity to do so. I only wish that as a teenager someone had explained all this as plainly to me as I have here, because it might have helped me make better choices. I also wish I'd have known how much God cared for me. Many scriptures testify to that fact and I wish I'd have known to rely on them to help me. (I've provided a list of the ones I've found helpful in the back of the book.)

God understands our weaknesses and has made a way for us to escape temptation. The Bible says in James 4:7: "Submit yourselves, therefore to God. Resist the devil, and he will flee from you." The Old Testament account of Joseph is a perfect example of what we should do when confronted with the temptation to sin sexually. Hear his words to Potiphar's wife: "My master has withheld nothing from me except you, because you are his wife. How then could I do such a wicked thing and sin against God?"—Genesis 39:9. Day after day she tempted him, but Joseph refused to go to bed with her and avoided her. The last time she tried to lure Joseph, she grabbed his cloak, and he ran out of the house, leaving his cloak in her hand. Running from temptation is not a sign of weakness, but strength. You don't owe anything to anyone who is tempting you to sin—and it is best to burn all bridges behind you so that you cannot be tempted by that situation again.

Since sin starts in our mind, we are admonished to "take captive every thought to make it obedient to Christ", in 2 Corinthians 10:5. We can memorize scripture so that at any point of weakness we have it at our disposal—Jesus Himself countered the temptations He endured with scripture. We should also put on the whole armor of God listed in Ephesians 6. Overcoming temptation takes effort but it is possible.

Just as a rock in the middle of rapids cannot escape the constant barrage of raging water, so an illegitimate child cannot escape the effects of the parents' sin. We never disobey without it affecting other people. There is, of course, forgiveness with God. If we find ourselves guilty of improper behavior, we don't have to continually bear that shame; God has provided through Jesus atonement for each and every one of the sins we have ever committed or will commit. He died once for all and if we are His, we can do what 1 John 1:9 instructs us to do: "If we confess our sins, He is faithful and just to forgive us our sins, and to cleanse us from all unrighteousness." We should not let this be an excuse to continue in sin, however; just as Jesus told the woman caught in adultery, we should, "Go and sin no more."

CHAPTER 17

THE CHOICE

To the woman who finds herself in the position of being pregnant and not married, I want to reiterate that abortion is not the answer. My mother chose to have me despite her bleak circumstances, and God has prevailed in our lives and even used it for good. Everything was harder than it had to be, but God brought us through. Who knows what that child might become? The researcher who finds the cure for some merciless disease? The missionary who God sends out into the harvest? The mother who raises your grandchildren in the nurture and admonition of the Lord? And before these, a human being, created in the image of God Himself.

I am familiar with a few women who have had an abortion. Abortion providers do not tell the women they serve of the devastation wrought by it. There are emotional, spiritual, and physical consequences. A woman's inability to forgive herself and resulting self-hatred can actually cause her body to turn against and attack itself with life-threatening disease. This is not just a scenario, it's reality for someone I know.

Another person has become an alcoholic in an attempt to dull the pain of her guilt. *Abortion is dangerous to mothers.* It is never the right answer.

If you have had an abortion, are you guilt-ridden still? Or have you laid that burden down at the cross, being forgiven by God and also forgiving yourself? Jesus knew every sin we would ever commit before we committed them, and agreed to take our punishment before the beginning of time: "This grace was given us in Christ Jesus before the beginning of time, but it has now been revealed through the appearing of our savior, Christ Jesus, who has destroyed death and has brought life and immortality to light through the gospel."—2 Timothy 1:9,10; "He forgave us all our sins, having cancelled the written code, with its regulations, that was against us and stood opposed to us; He took it away, nailing it to the cross. And having disarmed the powers and authorities, He made a public spectacle of them, triumphing over them by the cross." —Colossians 2:13-15. 1 John 1:9 states: "If we confess our sins, he is faithful and just to forgive us our sins, and to cleanse us from all unrighteousness." If God, who is greater than all (John 10:29), has removed our transgressions as far as the east is from the west (Psalm 103:12), who are we to not forgive ourselves? If we do not forgive ourselves, it is as if we are saying we are greater than God!

CHAPTER 18

FORGIVENESS

If someone had told me I was going to grow spiritually during the process of writing this small book, I would have believed it. But if someone had told me how radically my view of life and myself would be changed, I'd have laughed, unbelieving.

Until recently, I viewed life through the lens of the Law. Meaning, I knew Jesus died for me on the cross for the pardon of my sins. I accepted it; I wasn't going to hell. But there was this pressure to perform—to live up to what others expect a Christian to be. And when you live like that, under rules that no one can keep, you become cynical and judgmental and there is no joy like the kind the Bible talks about.

Since the start of this book, I have come to learn so much more about exactly what Christ did for me (and for all believers). About His mission. And it has radically changed how I view things, which in turn has radically changed my thought process, and consequently, my behavior. *You see, I discovered grace alone. And that has made all the difference.*

As I look back, I can see that God started this process years ago, only I didn't fully accept it. Maybe I couldn't accept it then, because I sure didn't get it. But now that I *do* get it, I want others to get it too. For years and years, I was the older brother in the story of the Prodigal. I was the one who stood outside the party and refused to go in, because I thought I was better than my brother who had just come traipsing back from the world's pigsty (Luke 15:11-32). But through Bible study, circumstances, sermons, articles, and a couple of really good books, God showed me that I was, in fact, worse than the younger brother. It all started with a prayer: "Lord, why don't I like people?" Yep. That was my question. And boy, did I ever get an answer. God dragged me to His spiritual mirror and had me take a good, long look at my own reflection.

During this process, I gained an idea of what the Hebrew patriarch, Jacob, must have endured during that epic wrestling match. I did not want to admit that my problem was a superiority complex. A pride issue. And so I dug in my heels. God might as well have said, "Okay. Be stubborn all you want, but I'm not giving you anything new to chew on until you give; oh, and by the way, you are going to feel horrible on the inside." For a person like me who has to have all sorts of mental stimulation when it comes to the spiritual, that is like a jail sentence. "Wait, what? God, you mean you're just going to let me twist in the wind?" Silence. I didn't get anything new out of my Bible study, and in fact, everything I read irked the daylights out of me. And I stubbornly dug in, fortifying my wrong beliefs and justifying them in my mind to the point that my stomach churned every time I thought about it.

You know God has a way of driving a point home. I can always tell when He's focusing on something He wants changed in me because I encounter it everywhere. Somewhere in the midst of my alternating anger and self-pity, I read enough materials (all ironically dealing with the last thought with which God left me) that I started to cave. And eventually I tapped out of the match and said, "You know what, God, you are right. I am the older brother. I am proud. I am judgmental. Good grief, I'm dangerously close to being a *Pharisee.*"

Once we got past that episode, God began showing me all kinds of new things. I walked into church on Sunday and they were just starting to study the entire book of Ephesians. Right off the bat, the pastor said, "If you are tired of doing, just *stop!*" It was as if God had showered a palpable form of His grace on me that day. What a relief I felt! It was like being set free from bondage, and that infernal gnawing in my gut that had plagued me when I thought I wasn't doing enough to please others disappeared.

Through the teaching on Ephesians, I have been reminded that none of us is spiritually superior; we are all, in fact, dead in sin before Christ raises us from spiritual death. Not half alive floating in a life preserver, but face-down-dead on the bottom of the ocean. Now, I knew that before, because I'd read it many times in scripture. But for some reason this time it oozed way down deep into my soul. In the wondrous way in which God weaves things together, He perfectly timed this to coincide with what I was learning at Bible study and books I'd bought to read. This did a lot to change the way I looked at myself. My superiority complex finally crumbled under the weight of the truth.

For the first time in my life, God's love became alive to me. Oh, I knew what the Bible said about it, I believed it existed, heard it preached on all my life, told others about it, but this time I've gotten a glimpse of the size of it. It is enormous. I believe it is an answer to Paul's prayer in Ephesians: "For this reason I kneel before the Father, from whom His whole family in heaven and on earth derives its name. I pray that out of His glorious riches He may strengthen you with power through His spirit in your inner being, so that Christ may dwell in your hearts through faith. And I pray that you, being rooted and established in love, may have power together with all the saints, to grasp how wide and long and high and deep is the love of Christ, and to know this love that surpasses knowledge—that you may be filled to the measure of all the fullness of God."—Ephesians 3:14-19

What does this have to do with forgiveness? Everything! Once you understand all these things— your own depravity, and the love that God still has for you in spite of it, and the sacrifice He made for you, and agreed to make for you before the foundation of the world, you can then operate from a position that allows you to truly forgive, in the Bible's sense of the word. We can't fall for the popular theme that's run amok nowadays: "Forgive for your own sake." That's a selfish form of forgiveness. We forgive because Christ forgave us. "Freely you have received, freely give."— Matthew 10:8. We forgive for Christ's sake and out of thankfulness for what He's done for us..

When I consider that Christ left His infinite riches in Heaven and became poor, so that I might become rich; that He lived the perfect life that I could not; that He agonized in the Garden of Gethsemane about the possibility of there being another way to redeem mankind, but submitted to His Father's will; that on top of the physical pain He suffered on the cross, He became sin for me, absorbed all of the Father's wrath so that I wouldn't have to, and endured separation from God so that I would never have to suffer that separation; that He rose from the dead so that I will not see death, I have no response but to be willing to obey.

There's an old Hymn written by Isaac Watts in 1707 called *When I Survey the Wondrous Cross* that sums it up well:

When I survey the wondrous cross
On which the Prince of glory died,
My richest gain I count but loss
And pour contempt on all my pride.

Forbid it, Lord, that I should boast,
Save in the death of Christ, my God;
All the vain things that charm me most,
I sacrifice them to his blood.

See, from his head, his hands, his feet,
Sorrow and love flow mingled down.
Did e'er such love and sorrow meet,
Or thorns compose so rich a crown.

Were the whole realm of nature mine,
That were an offering far too small;
Love so amazing, so divine,
Demands my soul, my life, my all.[11]

CHAPTER 19

IS GOD YOUR FATHER?

Have you come to realize that you cannot call God Father because you do not know Him nor does He know you? Jesus said, "I am the good shepherd; I know my sheep and my sheep know me."—John 10:14. He also said, "The man who enters by the gate is the shepherd of his sheep. The watchman opens the gate for him, and the sheep listen to his voice. He calls his own sheep by name and leads them out. When he has brought out his own, he goes on ahead of them, and his sheep follow him because they know his voice."—John 10:2-4. There is a way that you can, but you must repent (turn away) from your sin and put your faith in Christ and what he accomplished in His work on the cross.

- God is holy and cannot coexist with sin: "Your eyes are too pure to look on evil; you cannot tolerate wrong."—Habakkuk 1:13
- All are sinners separated from God until they've been reconciled to Him through Christ, and ALL have sinned: "There is no one righteous, not even one; there is no one who understands,

no one who seeks God."—Romans 3:10; "...for all have sinned and fall short of the glory of God..." —Romans 3:23

- The penalty for sin is death: "For the wages of sin is death, but the gift of God is eternal life in Christ Jesus our Lord." Romans 6:23

- Jesus is the only way to the Father: "For there is one God and one mediator between God and men, the man Christ Jesus, who gave Himself as a ransom for all men—the testimony given in its proper time."—1 Timothy 2:5,6

- Jesus lived the sinless life that we could not; God required a blameless sacrifice: "For we do not have a high priest who is unable to sympathize with our weaknesses, but we have one who has been tempted in every way, just as we are—yet was without sin." —Hebrews 5:15

- Jesus paid our sin debt that we could not pay by taking our punishment, God's wrath poured out on Him on the cross: "...so Christ was sacrificed once to take away the sins of many people..."—Hebrews 9:28

- When we accept Christ's payment on our behalf, God counts us righteous: "God made Him who had no sin to be sin for us, so that in Him we might become the righteousness of God."—2 Corinthians 5:21

- In Christ, we are new creations and should begin to display evidence of our faith: "Therefore, if anyone is in Christ, he is a new creation; the old has gone, the new has come! —2 Corinthians 5:17; "Jesus replied, 'If anyone loves Me, he will obey My teaching. My Father will love him, and We will come to him and make Our home with him. He who does not love Me will not obey My teaching.' " —John 14:23,24

- Because he lives, true believers in Him will live also: "But Christ has indeed been raised from the dead, the firstfruits of those who have fallen asleep. For since death came through a man, the resurrection of the dead comes also through a man. For as in Adam all die, so in Christ all will be made alive."—1 Corinthians 15:20-22

CHAPTER 20

THE SWORD

These are some of my favorite scriptures that are useful in combatting wrong thoughts. The Bible is the sword (Ephesians 6:17) of the believer, and is "mighty through God to the pulling down of strongholds." (2 Corinthians 10:4) I recommend a concordance that can be used to locate additional verses. Also, I don't want to underestimate the value of biblical counseling, or soul care, as the Puritans called it. Sometimes we need someone to come alongside and help us see that to which we are blinded, or to help us in prayer. Many times over the course of my life I have sought out counseling; my only warning would be to make sure you *know* that the counseling is biblical and the person doing it is qualified.

Children of God

Psalm 68:5,6: A father to the fatherless, a defender of widows, is God in His holy dwelling. God sets the lonely in families...

Hosea 14:3: ...for in You the fatherless find compassion.

Romans 8:15-17: For you did not receive a spirit that makes you a slave again to fear, but you received the Spirit of sonship. And by Him we cry, "Abba, Father." The Spirit Himself testifies with our spirit that we are God's children. Now if we are children, then we are heirs—heirs of God and co-heirs with Christ, if indeed we share in His sufferings in order that we may also share in His glory.

Galatians 3:26,27: You are all sons of God through faith in Christ Jesus, for all of you who were baptized into Christ have clothed yourself with Christ.

Galatians 4:4: But when the time had fully come, God sent His son, born of a woman, born under law, to redeem those under law, that we might receive the full rights of sons. Because you are sons, God sent the Spirit of His Son into our hearts, the Spirit who calls out, "Abba, Father." So you are no longer a slave, but a son; and since you are a son, God has made you also an heir.

1 John 3:1: Behold what manner of love the Father has bestowed on us, that we should be called children of God!

1 John 4:4: You, dear children, are from God and have overcome them, because the One who is in you is greater than the one who is in the world.

Hebrews 12:5-8: And you have forgotten that word of encouragement that addresses you as sons: "My son, do not make light of the Lord's discipline, and do not lose heart when He rebukes you, because the Lord disciplines those He loves, and He punishes everyone he accepts as a son." Endure hardship as discipline; God is treating you as sons. For what son is not disciplined by his father? If you are not disciplined (and everyone undergoes discipline), then you are illegitimate children and not true sons.

Other Helpful Verses

Proverbs 3:5,6: Trust in the LORD with all your heart and lean not on your own understanding; in all your ways acknowledge Him, and He will make your paths straight.

John 14:1-4: Do not let your hearts be troubled. Trust in God; trust also in Me. In my Father's house are many rooms; if it were not so, I would have told you. I am going there to prepare a place for you. And if I go and prepare a place for you, I will come back and take you to be with Me that you also may be where I am.

John 14:27: Peace I leave with you; My peace I give you. I do not give to you as the world gives. Do not let your hearts be troubled and do not be afraid.

Romans 8:1: Therefore, there is now no condemnation for those who are in Christ Jesus, because through Christ Jesus the law of the Spirit of life set me free from the law of sin and death.

Romans 8:26-28: In the same way, the Spirit helps us in our weakness. We do not know what we ought to pray for, but the Spirit Himself intercedes for us with groans that words cannot express. And He who searches our hearts knows the mind of the Spirit, because the Spirit intercedes for the saints in accordance with God's will. And we know that in all things God works for the good of those who love Him, who have been called according to His purpose.

Romans 8:33,34: Who will bring any charge against those whom God has chosen? It is God who justifies. Who is he that condemns? Christ Jesus, who died—more than that, who was raised to life—is at the right hand of God and is also interceding for us.

2 Corinthians 4:16-18: Therefore we do not lose heart. Even though our outward man is perishing, yet the inward man is being renewed day by day. For our light affliction, which is but for a moment, is working for us a far more exceeding and eternal weight of glory, while we do not look at the things which are seen, but at the things which are not seen. For the things which are seen are temporary, but the things which are not seen are eternal.

2 Corinthians 5:21: For He made Him who knew no sin to be sin for us, that we might become the righteousness of God in Him.

Hebrews 4:15,16: For we do not have a High Priest who cannot sympathize with our weaknesses, but was in all points tempted as we are, yet without sin. Let us therefore come boldly to the throne of grace, that we may obtain mercy and find grace to help in time of need.

Hebrews 13:5: ...God has said, "Never will I leave you; never will I forsake you." So we say with confidence, "The Lord is my Helper; I will not be afraid. What can man do to me?"

NOTES

1. *Charlie and the Chocolate Factory. Tim Burton. Warner Brothers. 2005. Film.*

2. *"The Monkees". Bob Rafelson, Bert Schneider. Raybert Productions, Screen Gems Television. Columbia Pictures Television. 12 September 1966-25 March 1968. Television.*

3. *The Monkees. "Daydream Believer". John Stewart. The Birds, The Bees, & The Monkees. Colgems. 1967. LP.*

4. *Mayer, John. "Daughters". Heavier Things. Columbia. 2004. MP3.*

5. *Gone With the Wind. Victor Fleming. MGM. 1939. Film.*

6. *Excerpt taken from: I See Grace Words and Music by: Jim Brady/ Tony Wood/ Barry Weeks. Brady House Publishing (BMI) New Spring a division of t Enterprises Inc. / Row J, Seat 9 Songs (ASCAP) Building Bridge, a division of Zomba Enterprises Inc. (BMI) Administered by Brentwood-Benson Music Publishing. All rights reserved. Used by permission.*

7. Cunningham, Ted. *Young and in Love: Challenging the Unnecessary Delay of Marriage*. Colorado Springs. David C. Cook. 2011. Print.

8. Hastings, Max. "Years of liberal dogma have spawned a generation of amoral, uneducated, welfare dependent, brutalized youngsters." *Mail Online*. Associated Newspapers Ltd. 12 August 2011. Web. 18 April 2013.

9. Martin JA, Hamilton BE, Ventura SJ, et al. Births: Final data for 2010. *National Vital Statistics Reports*; Vol. 61 No. 1, Hyattsville, MD: National Center for Health Statistics. 2012, p. 8, Table C.

10. Teetsel, Eric. "Why I Fight Against Same Sex Marriage". *Religion & Politics*. John C. Danforth Center on Religion & Politics. Washington University in St. Louis. 25 June 2013. Web. 30 June 2013.

11. Watts, Isaac. "When I Survey the Wondrous Cross". 1707. *Timeless Truths, Free Online Library*. Web. 24 May 2014

ACKNOWLEDGMENTS

I could not have written and published this book if it weren't for the following people, to whom many thanks are due: Dr. Sharon Hart May, Ph.D., thank you for the wildflower/rose metaphor. Phil and Mary Mason, for the realization that Father really does love us, and Phil in particular for the diamond illustration and application. Ken and Lisa Abraham for your sound, seasoned advice regarding writing and publishing (over a wonderful dinner). Thank you to my sweet husband for all his love, support, and effort in getting me access to the right people to help this project become a reality, and for his excellent fatherly example to my kids. He brings balance to my life and I love him dearly. My kids, for teaching me what a great father-child relationship should look like, and your unique personalities and our family interactions that help me understand God's love better. My mother, Martha Lister, for choosing life and taking the hard way out. My dear friend, Julie Pardue, for being a sounding board, a great support, and prayer warrior, the iron against which my iron is sharpened. Julie Ziglar Norman, for the wonderful support and editing. Peggy Palser, for the additional help dotting my Is and crossing my Ts. And finally, God the Father, Jesus the Son, and God the Holy Spirit for your love and dedication to a fallen humanity, who, in spite of our sin, You love anyway.

THE LOVE AFFAIR WITH SAND, SEASHELLS,
AND SALTY WATER STARTED EARLY.

About the Author

Vicki Booth is mom to two homeschooling boys and one homeschool graduate. She is the wife of Gospel singer Michael Booth of the Booth Brothers. Currently she spends her time with her sons, two Miniature Schnauzers, one parakeet, and Michael (when he's not on the road). She regularly attends Bible Study Fellowship International in an effort to know the Father better. Formerly a graphic artist, she worked for Dobbs Publishing Group in Lakeland, FL. She studied graphic art at Tampa Technical Institute and fine art at the University of Tampa.

Vicki resides in Spring Hill, Tennessee, but misses her home, the Sunshine State, immensely. You can sometimes find her daydreaming about palm trees and sand, or painting whatever subject she feels like painting. *The Wildflower* is her first book.